MAKE IT SOUND

Gillian Wills

CONTENTS

Oxford University Press, Music Department, Walton Street, Oxford OX2 6DP

Introduction

The two main objectives of *Make it Sound* are the presentation and discussion of musical concepts and the provision of material for classroom music. The six topics — Pop, Reggae, Soul, Rock'n' Roll, Classical and Jazz — carefully selected for their general appeal to the age range of 11 to 14 years — represent a distinct musical style, and have three simple arrangements. Each topic is arranged in the following way:

a a brief survey to introduce the musical style;

b three arrangements, each with its own introduction;

c an ideas section including a number of suggestions for follow-up activities — classroom music-making, discussion and comprehension. This ideas section allows teacher and pupil to explore the musical concepts in *Make it Sound*, notably Melody, Harmony, Rhythm and Tone colour. These concepts and elements are also outlined in the following diagram in the order in which they appear in each topic. *Make it Sound* can be used sequentially or teachers can select topics on an individual basis.

The arrangements

Each arrangement has three parts, referred to as the tune **A1** (harmony part) and **A2** (bass line). Guitar chord symbols are also given and can be used as an additional part if players sound the indicated chord root in crotchet beats or in a rhythm of their own choice. These arrangements are primarily intended for classroom instruments in general use and therefore the range of notes is limited to those shown below. Many of the parts can be played on standard instruments. B flat parts are included in the back of the book as it is hoped that all pupils, whether or not they are learning to play a standard instrument, can use the book and become involved in classroom music-making. The unusual combinations of instruments, producing a variety of tone colour, and the conscious rejection of the orthodox reproduction of musical styles enables all pupils to participate in classroom music-making whatever their personal skills and also allows the maximum use of available instruments in the school.

Notes you need

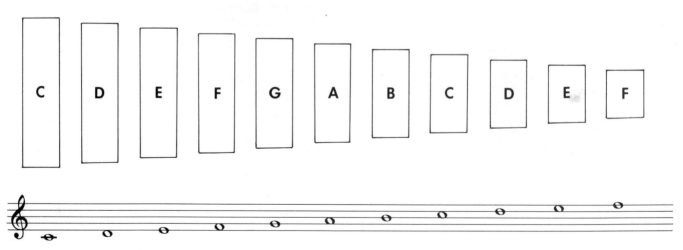

Concepts

Skills and related ideas

Topics	Melody	Rhythm	Harmony	Form	Tone colour	Dynamics
Pop	tune note scale key (G major) D minor) key signature ♭ flat sign ♯ sharp sign ♮ natural sign stepwise, leaps and repeated notes hook riff	rhythm beat bar time signature tie	accompaniment balance	form in a pop song repeat marks 1st, 2nd and 3rd time bars		
Reggae	C major E minor A minor	accent rest	3 note chord (triad) root, 3rd and 5th of a chord singing in harmony	call and response coda	Tone colour falsetto	getting softer
Soul	F major sequence low/high	triplet	4 note (7th) chord	12 bar chord pattern		getting louder
Rock'n' roll	flattened 7th accompanying tune bass pattern built on the root, 5th and 6th notes of a chord					
Classical	phrase theme			symphony minuet music in 3 sections alberti bass theme & variations ground bass		Dynamics loud f soft p
Jazz	"blue" notes	syncopation	4 note (6th) chord	improvisation break fill in tunes vamp walking bass		

POP

Sting and The Police in concert

Popular music or pop has been described as the music which much of the world listens to most of the time. Pop exists on records and although other kinds of music are also recorded, there is a difference. In jazz, for example, records capture performances but in pop, performances try to recreate the sound of records. Pop singers and groups compete to sell as many records as possible and to create for themselves an individual style. The sounds and instruments used in the backing of a record contribute to a pop musician's style, the type of songs recorded and the way in which these songs are sung. Some of pop music's special qualities are bright memorable **tunes** and an emphasis on **beat** and **rhythm**.

The beat and rhythm

It is the drummer in a pop group who holds the music together whilst moving it along by the beat and rhythm. The steady and continuous beat is like the regular ticking of a clock and it can always either be heard or felt by the listener. The rhythms (the arrangements of sounds and silences into sound patterns) decorate the beat. The drummer not only sets and maintains the beat but also plays a variety of rhythms in combination with it. By changing the speed of the beat the drummer can make the song faster or slower and can often be heard leading the music on into a new section. Sometimes, as in the case in *Maid of Orleans* by Orchestral Manoeuvres in the Dark, a percussion synthesizer is used to mechanically pound out the beat.

The tune

To make a hit record a songwriter tries to compose a tune which is simple yet catchy enough for listeners to remember — a tune which they will want to hear again. A **tune** is a chain of different notes, heard one at a time and arranged in a way that sounds well. Pop performers such as The Police, Orchestral Manoeuvres in the Dark and Neil Young often write their own songs. Most pop songs last no longer than three minutes and are organized in a way that gives a song a clear and recognizable shape. There is generally an **introduction** to the singing, one or two **instrument-only sections**, several **verses** followed by a singable **chorus** and an **ending**.

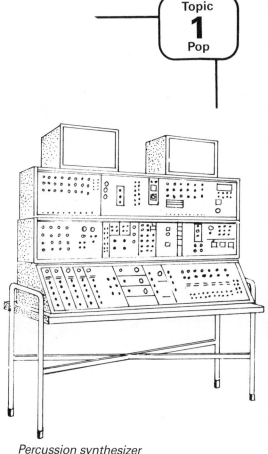

Percussion synthesizer

The accompaniment

The instrumental backing of a pop record is known as its **accompaniment**. Of little interest on its own, an accompaniment supports the tune and often brings out the meaning of the words and gives the song character. The instruments which generally accompany pop songs are played through amplifiers and heard through loud speakers. They include the electric guitar, organ and piano as well as other instruments like the violin, flute, saxophone, trumpet and mouth organ. The range of sound effects in pop music is enormous, especially since the introduction of synthesizers. A synthesizer can produce, imitate or change sounds electronically. Many groups like The Police use synthesized sounds. Orchestral Manoeuvres in the Dark mainly use rhythm machines, tape recorders as well as synthesizers to make up their music. Other electronic gadgets like the fuzz box and reverberation unit are used in connection with the electric guitar to produce sound distortion or echo effects.

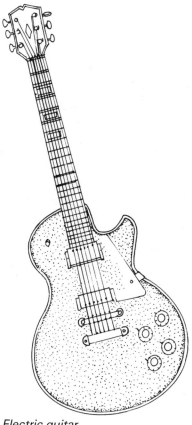

Electric guitar

The recording studio

Because records are so important in pop, record producers have a great responsibility, for by the means of a wide range of equipment available at a recording studio they can affect a recording in many different ways. In a studio each voice, sound or instrument is recorded on its own section of tape or track. If after listening to a recording, the singer is being drowned by the accompaniment, the volume can be turned up on the singer's track until the correct **balance** has been achieved. As well as adjusting the volume level of each track according to the desired overall effect, the producer can also add extra sounds to a particular track, alter the sound of instruments or remove unwanted sounds from a recording.

Maid of Orleans

The synthesizer-styled band Orchestral Manoeuvres in the Dark recorded *Maid of Orleans* in 1981.

Beats are heard or felt in groups of two, three or four. Beat groupings on written music are separated by **bar lines**. The first beat in a group of beats is stressed. In most pop music there are four beats in a bar, but in *Maid of Orleans* the beats are heard as

STRONG   weak   weak;

in other words, there are **three** beats in each bar. A2 consists of repeated notes marking out the beat.

Orchestral Manoeuvres in the Dark — a synthesizer-styled band

At the beginning of a piece of music just after the **treble clef** sign 𝄞 a set of figures known as the **time signature** tells the players how the beats are grouped. It can look like this $\frac{2}{4}$, or $\frac{3}{4}$ and $\frac{4}{4}$. The top figure tells a player how many beats there are in each bar.

In the tune and A1 there are curved lines connecting two notes of the same level or **pitch**. These lines are known as **ties** and indicate that the note is only to be sounded once and held for the combined length of both notes.

Suggested instrumentation

Tune Soprano melodica or metallophone, glockenspiel, guitar, flute, descant recorder, oboe, flute or violin.

A1 Alto melodica or metallophone, descant recorder, guitar, flute and violin.

A2 Bass xylophone, bass guitar, lower pitched notes on piano, cello or double bass.

In A2 both lower sounding Ds and Cs are used as well as higher sounding Ds and Cs. Be careful not to confuse both kinds when you play this part on a bass xylophone or piano.

lower C   higher C   lower D   higher D

Plan of the song
Instrument only section
Verse
Instrument only section
Verse
Instrument only section

At bar 64 do what the sign :‖ says and repeat from the beginning.

Maid of Orleans (Waltz Joan of Arc)

Ideas

1 Divide into three groups. Each group can learn either the tune, A1 or A2.

   a The group playing the tune can sing in the required passages instead of playing.

   b Some members of the group playing A2 can play the part as written, and the others can play the given notes in each bar to different rhythms, for example:

   c Appoint a group of rhythm players, one player to provide the beat and a few other players who can make up rhythms to decorate the beat.

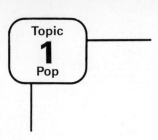
2 Make a recording of your playing and singing of *Maid of Orleans*.
  a Listen to the recording and decide if the balance is right between the tune or singing and the accompaniment. If the accompaniment is drowning the tune or singing you will need to:
  ask the accompaniment players to play softer;
  tell the tune players and singers to perform louder;
  position the cassette player or microphone nearer the singing and the instruments playing the tune;
  listen to the rhythm players. They may be performing too loudly.
3 Create a piece of music with two sections, the first with two beats in a bar and the second with three beats in a bar.
4 Give everyone an untuned percussion instrument and sit in a circle. One person should play a steady beat of three *throughout* the activity. Each member of the circle in turn can create a rhythm to fit with the beat and repeat it continuously until asked to stop. Choose a leader who can indicate to the players when to start or stop, play in various combinations, altogether or one at a time.

  Tape record this activity. If you want particular rhythms to be in the foreground of the music choose someone to hold the cassette recorder or microphone near the particular rhythm(s) required to stand out in the music as it is recorded.

drum

triangle

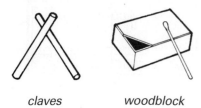

claves   *woodblock*

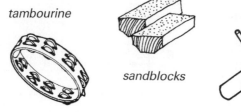

tambourine

sandblocks

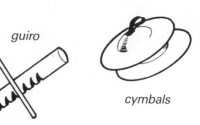

guiro

cymbals

5 Listen to extracts from several pop records. Can you tell how the beats are grouped?

Recommended listening

Architecture and Morality   Orchestral Manoeuvres in the Dark
The Man Machine   Kraftwerk
Equinoxe   Jean-Michel Jarre
Discreet Music   Brian Eno
Vienna   Ultravox

Heart of gold

Neil Young is well known as a singer and songwriter who records his own songs. *Heart of Gold* recorded by him in 1972 became a commercially successful Top Ten hit.

This pop tune, and most other tunes too, are based on a particular series of eight notes called **scales**. Notes are called by the letter names A B C D E F G and each note has its own position on the musical stave. These are the notes you will use in this book.

Heart of Gold uses the following scale as the basis of its music:

A feeling of **key** is created when a tune is made from the notes in a certain scale. There are many kinds of scales; in pop most tunes are based on either major, minor or modal scales. A quick way of finding out which notes are used in a tune, is by looking at the key signature. This occurs after the treble clef sign in the form of a number of **sharps** and **flats** . A note with a sharp sign ♯ is half a step higher than the same note without it. A note with a flat ♭ sign is half a step lower. When a key signature shows a sharp or a flat on a particular note's position, then that note is to be sharpened or flattened throughout the song, unless a natural sign ♮ is printed beside the note in question and then it is played without a sharp or flat.

Tunes can move up or down by step,

by leaps,

or they can use repeated notes:

Singer-songwriter Neil Young

Suggested instrumentation

Tune Descant recorder, soprano xylophone, metallophone or melodica, guitar and glockenspiel.
A1 Descant recorder, alto metallophone, xylophone or melodica and guitar.
A2 Bass guitar, bass xylophone or metallophone and lower range of piano.

Heart of Gold

Moderately and simply

1. I wan-na live, I wan-na give, I've been a min-er for a Heart of Gold. It's these ex-press-ions

I nev-er give that keep me search-in' for a Heart of Gold,— And I'm get-tin' old.

I've been to Hol-ly-wood,— I've been to Redwood, I'd cross the ocean for a

Ideas

1 Learn to play the tune, A1 and A2.
2 Sing the song and accompany it with a small group of instruments playing A1 and A2.
3 Make up another part to go with this arrangement. One way of doing this is to make use of the chord names placed above the bars on the music. If the chord indicated is D minor, play D; or if the chord is B♭, play B♭, and so on. Play these notes to suitable rhythms.
4 Make up two or three rhythms to play on untuned percussion instruments. Experiment until you find rhythms which suit the mood of the song.
5 Divide into groups and work towards a performance of *Heart of Gold*. Consider the following:
   a Which instrument(s) should play the tune?
   b Will it be an instrument-only performance?
   c If you are to include singing, will you have one or several singers?
   d Which instruments will play A1 and A2?
   e Will you include rhythm parts for untuned percussion to play?
   f Will you appoint a leader to the group?
6 Tape record your performance and ask another group to assess it with the following points in mind;
   a Do you start and end together?
   b Can the singing or tune be heard clearly?
   c Is the speed steady or does it get faster or slower?
7 Make up a tune using five of the notes from the scale on which this song is based. Include a higher and a lower note D, repeated notes, notes moving by step and leaps in the tune you make up.
8 Listen to any pop song you like. Does the tune ever use repeated notes, move in leaps or go up or down by step?
9 Listen to a pop song. Write down the words of the chorus if there is one.
   a Does the accompaniment change during the chorus?
   b Does the drummer push the music on towards the chorus or not?
10 Describe in detail the order of events in the plan or shape of a pop song in terms of verses, choruses and instrument-only sections.

Recommended listening

Harvest   Neil Young (includes *Heart of Gold*)
Comes a time   Neil Young

Can't stand losing you

In 1978, The Police recorded their first album, *Outlandos D'Amour*, which included the songs *Roxanne* and *Can't stand losing you*; these songs became Top Ten hits. Pop songs which get into the charts almost always contain a **hook**, that is, a short catchy tune repeated several times in a record. Sometimes hooks are set to the words from which a song's title is derived. The hook in this song occurs to the words, 'can't stand losing you' from bars 17-23. The Police have an individual style which is immediately recognizable. Apart from using hooks, **riffs** are often to be heard as an important part of accompaniments in their songs. A riff is a constantly repeated short tune, often of only a few notes, which forms a continuous accompaniment to the main tune.

This is an example of a riff:

The Police's music has also borrowed elements from **reggae** in its rhythms (see Topic 2, Reggae) and frequent emphasis on the bass guitar and drums.

The Police in the recording studio

Suggested instrumentation

Tune Soprano xylophone, metallophone or melodica, glockenspiel, guitar and oboe.

A1 Descant recorder, flute, guitar, oboe, alto or tenor metallophones and xylophones.

A2 Bass metallophone or xylophone and bass guitar.

First, second and third time bars
These sometimes occur at the end of a section, chorus or verse to be repeated. First time through, the first group of notes is played; when repeating the section, the second group of notes is played and the third time through the third group of notes is performed.

Dal Segno al Fine = go back to the sign 𝄋, *Fine* marks the place at which to finish.

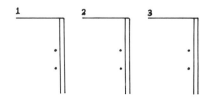

Can't stand losing you

BRIDGE SECTION LEADING TO CHORUS

Guess this is our last good-bye and you don't care so I won't cry and

you'll be sor - ry when I'm dead and all this guilt will be on your head I

Ideas

1 Learn to play the tune, A1 and A2.
2 Learn to sing the song.
3 A song can vary in the way it sounds according to how it is accompanied. Divide into groups and work towards as individual a performance of *Can't stand losing you* as possible.
4 Listen to several endings on pop records. The ending in this arrangement is very short. Try and make up a longer and more interesting ending.

5 Divide into groups of three. Make up a riff using the notes D C F. When you are satisfied with your riff, play it continuously so that someone else in the group can make up a tune to go with it.

   a Make up another riff this time with the notes A G C. Now make up a tune to suit the new riff.

   b Decide how many times each riff should be repeated and play each riff and tune alternately.

   c You could add a rhythm to be played on a tambourine, woodblock or drum.

   d Tape record your performance. Listen to it and decide if the speed remains the same throughout the performance.

   e Can you hear the tune clearly?

   f Do you play your parts at the right times?

   g Is the change from the first riff to the second smooth or is there an interruption to the flow of the music?

6 Listen to several pop records. Identify any snippets of tune you particularly like. Do you think these are hooks or not?

7 Listen to several records by The Police. Write down a few characteristics of their style.

8 Listen to another record by The Police.

   a Do you hear a riff?

   b If you can hear one on what instrument is it being played?

   c Is the riff played continuously throughout the record, or does it stop for a time and then reoccur?

Recommended listening

Outlandos D'Amour   The Police
Regatta de Blanc   The Police
Zenyatta Mondatta   The Police
Ghost In The Machine   The Police

REGGAE

Bob Marley — the king of reggae

Reggae, a music from Jamaica, began in the sixties and is a blend of African, Soul and Caribbean music. Bands such as Bob Marley and the Wailers, Toots and the Maytals and Black Slate have contributed to reggae's popularity. Once you hear reggae, you will recognize it immediately because of its unique sound. Reggae has distinctive rhythms, accompaniments, a generally booming bass sound, its own singing style and **dub** (see opposite).

Reggae rhythm

Reggae is characterized by a slow deliberate beat divided into groups or bars of four. There is an emphasis or accent on the second and fourth beats. It sounds rather like *mm — chk mm — chk*, and in musical notes would be shown as follows  is the musical sign for **accent**. This rhythm has been described as the reggae heartbeat, and is usually stressed by the bass drum of the drum kit. As reggae developed the heartbeat rhythm slowed down. The first kind of reggae was called **ska** and was played at a fast pace. *My Boy Lollipop* is a ska record. As the *mm — chk* rhythm is always constant, other different rhythms are played on hand drums and other percussion instruments to decorate the basic rhythm and to provide variety. Reggae rhythm is now frequently used by most groups such as The Police with recordings such as *Reggatta de Blanc*.

Chords

Reggae accompaniments are made up of **chords**. A chord is the sounding of two or more notes together. In reggae the accompanying chords are very often played on the second and fourth beats by the rhythm guitarist who plays them with short, rapid strokes across the strings. They can also be played by a keyboard player on either the electric piano or organ:

The bass

The lowest sounding strand in music is known as the **bass** and in reggae is very important. It is played by the bass guitarist who makes up short, catchy tunes usually based on or around the notes which make up the accompanying chords. The bass part is always noticeable and you can hear it very clearly whenever there is no singing on a record.

Singing styles

Singing styles range from harsh to smooth to gentle. Bob Marley had a change-able voice, which could rage and sound sentimental all within the same song. Often a backing group of singers is used; this will either join in with the lead singer on certain words to highlight their meaning and build up excitement, or else will reply to lines sung by the lead singer with a fuller vocal sound. The lead guitar and sometimes the trombone, melodica or saxophone will respond to and weave in and out of the singer's tunes. The words are often angry, protesting about poverty in Jamaica, the days of slavery or black inequality.

Dub

Reggae records are generally cut with two versions of the same song. The A side of a record features the singer and instrumental backing and the B side presents only the backing, sometimes with electronic sound effects. A recording featuring only the backing tracks is known as **dub**.

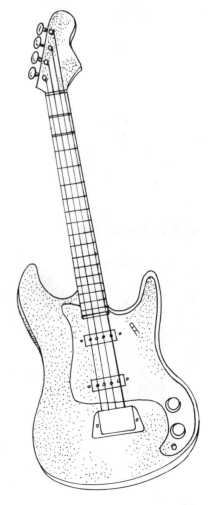

The bass guitar

Topic
2
Reggae

My boy lollipop

In 1964, a ska song, *My Boy Lollipop*, was recorded by a young Jamaican called Millie Small. Ska is a fast kind of reggae which often features brass instruments like the trumpet, trombone and french horn. This song became the first ska hit to reach the British charts and it prompted the release of a rapid succession of Jamaican and British-based ska records.

Music is not only made up of sound but also of silences. Silences in written music are indicated by signs called **rests**. Rests vary in length, they can last for a quarter or half of a beat, for one beat, two or four beats. They look like this:

The tune is broken up by rests. When you play or sing this part you will need to notice and recognize these rests.

Millie Small, who recorded
My Boy Lollipop

Suggested instrumentation

Tune Descant recorder, soprano melodica, xylophone or metallophone, glockenspiel, guitar and oboe.

A1 Descant recorder, alto or tenor metallophones and xylophones, violin, guitar and flute.

A2 Bass xylophone and bass guitar as well as the lower range of the piano.

My Boy Lollipop

Ideas

1 Learn to play this arrangement.
2 Learn to sing this song.
3 There is a short tune of three notes which can be played as part of the accompaniment. It occurs at the end of certain lines like this:

Play this tune in the following bars; 3, 5, 11, 13, 27 and 29.

a A trumpet or clarinet player can play the same tune on these notes:

4 Try playing the accompanying chords in alternative ways. For example, they can be played to this rhythm:

and like this:

or you can play notes from the chords separately in this kind of pattern:

5 Work on an ending. For instance, each repetition of bars 34 and 35 could get softer, or, arrange for instruments to stop playing in turns.

6 Divide into groups. Using body sounds like finger snapping, clapping or stamping and percussion instruments such as the tambourine, woodblock and drum, select someone to sound this rhythm ♩ ♩ ♩ ♩ . The other members listen to it and take it in turns to create other rhythms which decorate and add to the first player's reggae rhythm.

a Choose a group to accompany an instrumental performance of *My Boy Lollipop*.

b Work out a rhythmic accompaniment to a reggae record.

c Try making up rhythms using only nonsense syllables. Someone should keep repeating *mm — chk mm — chk* in a rhythmical way as others make up word rhythms which fit or add to the basic word pattern.

7 Make up a piece of music based on sounds and silences. A leader can direct the beginnings and endings of the silences.

Amigo

If the tune of a song is repeated too often it becomes boring unless there is some variety. Variety is usually produced by introducing a second tune in the song and, then after a while returning to the first tune. In *Amigo*, a successful hit record of 1980 by Black Slate, the first tune occurs between bars 5 to 16. From bars 17 to 27 a new tune is introduced before the first tune re-occurs.

Once you know how to find the notes in a **chord** you will be able to make up your own reggae accompaniments and bass tunes. The notes in a chord include the note it is named after, so, the first or **root** note of the C chord will be C. On a xylophone or piano count up three notes from C.

C	D	E					
1	2	3					

You come to the note E which is the middle of the chord and known as the **third**. Now count up five notes from C.

C	D	E	F	G			
1	2	3	4	5			

The note G is a **fifth** and is the last note in a three-note chord. A chord of three notes is called a **triad** as it is made up of the root, the third and fifth notes from that root.

C	d	E	f	G			
1		3		5			

The triad of C

Black Slate in concert at the Marquee club in London

Suggested instrumentation

Tune Violin, oboe, descant recorder, soprano melodica, xylophone and metallophone, glockenspiel and guitar.

A1 Descant recorder, alto melodica, alto and tenor metallophones or xylophones and guitar.

A2 Bass guitar, bass metallophone and xylophone as well as the lower pitched notes of the piano.

Amigo

Ideas

1 Learn to play and sing *Amigo*.

2 **a** Play the triads of E minor   and D minor throughout the song

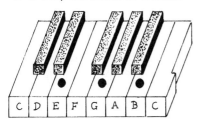 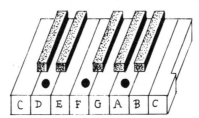

to this rhythm

  Share the notes in each triad between several xylophone, chime bar and metallophone players or play them on the piano or guitar.

  b Instead of sounding the notes in each triad together try playing them one after the other like this:

3 Using the notes in A1 sing the word *Amigo* in harmony with the lead singers when this song is sung.

4 Work on the ending of this song.

5 Tape record a combined singing and instrumental performance of *Amigo*.

  a Listen to the recording. Can you always hear the singing clearly or is the accompaniment occasionally too loud?

6 A typical arrangement of chords (or **chord progression**) in reggae is as follows:

  a Play this chord progression on guitars, xylophones, metallophones, chime bars or on the piano.

  b Divide into groups. Play the chords through while one player makes up a tune which sounds good with this accompaniment.

  c Make up some words for the tune.

  d Add some rhythms played on percussion instruments such as the tambourine or drum.

7 Listen to a reggae record and answer these questions.

  a Can you hear the bass part?

  b Does the bass part play continually or is it ever silent?

  c Do you hear one or several singers?

  d Which of these instruments can you hear? drum kit, hand-played drums, lead, rhythm or bass guitar, electric piano or organ, trombone and melodica.

  e How is variety achieved in this record?

Roots rock reggae

Bob Marley

The music of Bob Marley and The Wailers demonstrates a great variety of instrumental and vocal combinations of sound. Bob Marley was the group's lead singer and rhythm guitarist, and he wrote many of the group's songs. On many of his records a group of background singers or a vocal backing group accompany him singing different notes which blend in easily with the main tune. This is called singing in harmony. The notes the vocal backing group sing are from the song's chords.

Reggae bass lines are often built on or around the notes in the accompanying chords. The **root** and **fifth** of chords are often used. In *Roots, Rock, Reggae* the first chord is A minor. The bass line in the first bar can be made from the root A

and the fifth of that chord which is | A B C D E | Notes in a reggae

bass line are often repeated and can sound like this:

Another kind of bass line plays the notes in each chord as follows:

You can also use the note which comes before the *root* of each chord.

Suggested instrumentation

Tune Violin, flute, oboe, soprano melodica, metallophone or xylophone, glockenspiel and apart from bars 1-4 the descant recorder.

A1 Descant recorder, alto melodica, guitar and alto and tenor metallophones and xylophones.

A2 Bass guitar, bass xylophone and cello and double bass.

Roots, Rock, Reggae

31

Ideas

1 Learn to play this arrangement.
2 Work out the notes in the chords of A minor, D minor and E minor. Add these chords to the accompaniment.
3 The bass part in A2 is very simple and uses only the root of each chord. Make up an alternative bass part using the root and the fifth of each chord.
   Now make up a bass part using the note which comes immediately before the *root* of each chord.
4 Try and work out a *harmony* part which can be sung by a vocal backing group with the line 'Roots, rock, reggae — This a reggae music'.
5 Divide into groups and work out a *dub* section for bars 17 to 32.
   Play either A2 or a bass part you have made up and the appropriate chords. Using untuned percussion instruments make up some rhythms which sound well with this combination.
   a Play the arrangement through many times and include one or two of the worked out *dub* sections.
6 Listen to a Bob Marley record.
   a Can you hear a vocal backing group?
   b Do you hear any singing in harmony?
   c Are any of the lines sung by Bob Marley answered by a vocal backing group?
   d Can you hear the bass part?
   e Do you hear any repeated notes in the bass part?
7 Listen to a *dub* version of a record.
   a Do you notice snippets of the tune being played?
   b Is the bass playing with only untuned percussion instruments or are there other instruments playing as well?
8 Listen to another *dub* version of a record and try to make up a tune to play along with it.

Recommended listening

Rastaman Vibration   Bob Marley and the Wailers   Island, 1975
Exodus   Bob Marley and the Wailers   Island, 1976
Dub Duel   Kingdom Records   Island, 1976

SOUL

Michael Jackson in concert

Soul is dancing music with powerful rhythms and a foot-tapping beat. Soul performers often dance to simple routines as they sing their songs, which are inspired by a particular rhythm rather than a tune or a set of lyrics. As one soul musician put it, 'rhythm is basic, if you get that, that's what the people want'. Funky features on a soul record are brought out by pounding drum rhythms, jangling tambourines and percussive hand-clapping. Some soul songs also have the repetitive rumbling rhythm of a low sounding bass guitar riff. Words are not thought to be of much importance in soul songs; they are simple, often rhyme (as in, for example, 'movie star' and 'expensive car') and deal with the feelings of people in love. The word, 'love' is often in the title of the song as in the case of *I'm stone in love with you* and *Never knew love like this before*.

The roots of soul

Soul has been influenced both by **gospel** music and a style of singing known as **doo-wop**. Gospel is black religious music and soul has incorporated a well-known gospel characteristic, **call and response**. The **call** occurs when the lead singer sings a line, which is immediately answered by a group of singers who **respond** either by repeating the original line or by singing a different one. The response is often sung in harmony. Vocal harmony also played an important role in doo-wop music where instruments were rarely used. In doo-wop the tune, accompanying chords, bass line and rhythm parts were all sung by vocalists. Today, soul vocal groups like The Detroit Spinners, The Stylistics and solo artists like Stephanie Mills borrow from gospel and doo-wop music and use harmonizing accompaniments and vocal backing groups as an addition to their song's accompaniments.

french horn

trumpet

saxophone

Tone colour

In music, every instrument or voice has its own distinctive sound or **tone-colour**. The blending of instruments and voices in different combinations creates a never-ending source of tone-colours. A record producer ensures that combinations of tone-colours change during a record so that a listener will find the soul sound compelling and ear-catching. As you listen to a soul record you might hear any of the following tone-colours:

a a low sounding riff played on a bass guitar,

b a rhythm guitarist playing chords in a variety of rhythms,

c a higher sounding lead guitar playing tunes complementary to the singer's,

d tone-colours produced by the drum kit, such as the swishing of the hi-hat cymbal, crackling of the snare drum and the bass drum thumping,

e riffs played on brass instruments like the french horn, trumpet, or trombone,

f saxophone, or flute,

g smooth sounding violins,

h solo singer, female or male,

i voices singing in harmony.

drum kit

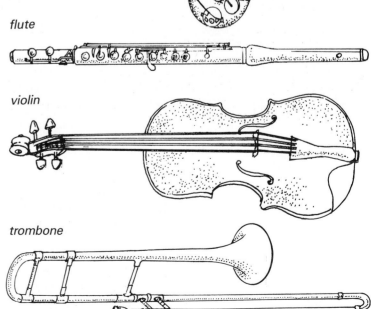

flute

violin

trombone

Never knew love like this before

Stephanie Mills is the latest in a long tradition of female soul singers, of whom Diana Ross is perhaps the most famous. The use of a **triplet** occurs in this song. Shown by a *3* above or below the notes, it means that three notes are to be played in the time of two. Triplets are often used in slow soul songs to give a lingering, relaxed feel to the music.

I nev - er knew

Much use is made in soul songs of the **seventh chord**. Seventh chords are shown on the music like this — G7, Dm7 or Em7. A seventh chord combines the usual three notes of a triad with the minor seventh note from the root of the chord.

The triad of G is

Look again at the scale of G and count up seven notes.

F♯ is the seventh note but it must be flattened in order to become the required **minor seventh**. The chord of G7 is:

Other seventh chords in this song are Em7 and Dm7.

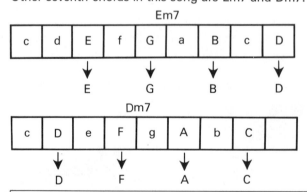

Suggested instrumentation

Tune Soprano melodica, metallophone and xylophone, guitar, piano, oboe and glockenspiel.

A1 Alto or tenor metallophones and xylophones, glockenspiel, guitar and oboe.

A2 Cello, bass guitar, lower range of piano and bass xylophone or metallophone.

Stephanie Mills — a soul singer in the tradition of Diana Ross

Never knew love like this before

3 You are my sunlight and my rain and time could never change   Repeat Chorus.
    What we share for ever more

Ideas

1 Learn to play this arrangement.

2 Divide into three groups. Each group can learn either the tune, A1 or A2. When each group has played their part successfully as part of a performance of the song, try singing the tune, A1 and A2. The tune can be sung to the words but the other groups could sing their parts to nonsense syllables such as *bop bop bee doo wah*, for example.

   a Tape record a performance of your doo-wop singing.

   b Listen to it and decide whether or not each group has managed to sing their part correctly.

3 Work towards a combined performance of singing and playing.

   a Make up a harmony part which can be sung with the tune. Use the root notes of the chords written above the music. If that is too easy, perhaps you can sing in harmony by ear or choose other notes from each chord as your harmony notes. For example, from the notes in the chord of G7 you can choose G, B, D or F. Experiment in each case to find the notes which sound best.

   b Play the chords on the guitar or the piano. Play each chord on the first beat of every bar like this:

   c When you can change chords easily, try playing them to a more interesting soul rhythm.

4 Divide into groups of five players. Four players should split the notes in various triads and seventh chords between them. Play through several chords in a random order. Test the fifth person in your group to see if he or she can hear the difference between a triad and a seventh chord.

   a Now play through this chord progression continuously.

   b Using the following notes take it in turns to make up a tune whilst the chord progression is played.

Recommended listening

Sweet Sensation   Stephanie Mills (includes *Never knew love like this before.*)

Black and White   The Pointer Sisters

Diana Ross Greatest Hits   Diana Ross

Aretha   Aretha Franklin

Cupid

The Detroit Spinners, who recorded Cupid

The Detroit Spinners are a well known vocal soul group. They have been making soul records since the 1960s but their most recent hit songs have been *Working my way back to you* and *Cupid*. In Cupid a tension is created in the opening chorus by a smooth sweeping tune moving mainly in leaps.

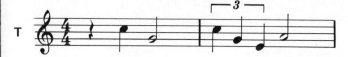

This tension is released in the verse by a bouncy tune using repeated notes which move up or down in steps.

Many soul records have such tensions and releases in either the chorus or the verse.

The riff in A2 is played as a **sequence**. When a tune is repeated and each repetition starts on a higher or lower note it is called a sequence. The riff in *Cupid* uses the first, third and fifth notes of a chord. For example, in Bar 1 the chord is C and the notes to be played are:

In Bar 2 the chord shown in Am and the notes to be played are:

Suggested instrumentation

Tune Descant recorder, soprano metallophone, xylophone and melodica, glockenspiel, oboe and guitar.

A1 Alto or tenor metallophones and xylophones, guitar and glockenspiel.

A2 Bass guitar, lower range of piano and bass xylophone or metallophone.

Cupid

1. I don't mean to bo-ther you but I'm in dis-tress ___ There's dan-ger of me los-ing all of
2. Cu-pid, if your ar-row makes her love strong for me ___ I pro-mise I will love her un-til

my hap-pi - ness ___ For I love a girl who does-n't know I ex-ist. ___
e - ter-ni - ty ___ I know 'tween the two of us her heart we can steal. ___

And this you can fix, Oh,
Help me if you will. ___

Ideas

1 Learn to play and sing this song.
2 Practise playing the riff in A2 starting on C, F, A and G.
  When you can do this easily you can play A2 just by following the chord names above each bar.
3 Make up a four-bar introduction to this song using the following chord progression:

4 Select new instruments to play during the verse so that there is some variety in tone-colour and the differences between the chorus tune and the verse tune will be highlighted.
5 Make up some rhythm parts on untuned percussion instruments to play during the chorus.
6 Sing A1 during the verse instead of playing it.
7 Experiment with some gimmicky sounds you could add to a performance of this song.
8 Tape record a performance of *Cupid*.
9 Assess your performance. Do you think that there are enough changes in tone-colour to make it sound interesting?
10 Listen to a soul record and answer these questions.
  a What kinds of tone-colours do you hear?
  b Do you notice a rhythmic bass guitar riff?
  c Is the tune for the verse different from the chorus tune?
  d If verse tune and chorus tune sound different what makes them sound unalike?
  e Is the chorus accompanied in a new way from the tune?
  f Do you hear any electronic sound effects?
  g Do you hear any seventh chords in the song?
  h Do you hear any percussive hand-clapping?
11 Make up a bass riff to play as a sequence to this chord progression:

Am7 / / / | D7 / / / | G7 / / / | C / / / |

Recommended listening

Love Trippin'   The Detroit Spinners

I'm stone in love with you

*The Stylistics, who recorded
I'm stone in love with you*

I'm stone in love with you was a popular hit in the 1970s and was recorded by a vocal soul group called The Stylistics. In soul there is a tendency for singers to sing notes which range from very low to very high. Male singers like Michael Jackson, Stevie Wonder and the lead singer of The Stylistics often sing **falsetto** — a man singing very high notes, beyond the normal range of his voice. Another soul characteristic is the singing of several notes to a single syllabled word like 'you', for example:

Stone   in   love with   you_____.

A short section added on to the end of this song rounds off the music and gives it a finished feel. Such finishing-off sections occur in all kinds of music and are called **codas**. In the codas of soul records, the performers often round off a song by singing snippets of the chorus tune changed slightly, or by repeating certain words and singing in new harmonies.

The seventh chords used in this song are C7 and Gm7.

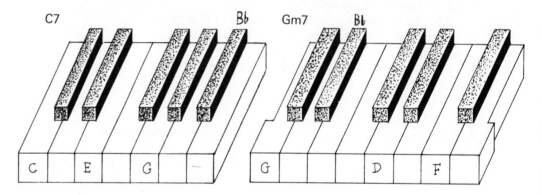

D.S. al coda = Go back to the beginning and play the coda.

Suggested instrumentation

Tune Guitar, descant recorder, oboe, soprano metallophones and xylophones and glockenspiel.

A1 Alto melodica, alto or tenor metallophone and xylophone.

A2 Bass guitar, cello, bass xylophone or metallophone.

I'm stone in love with you

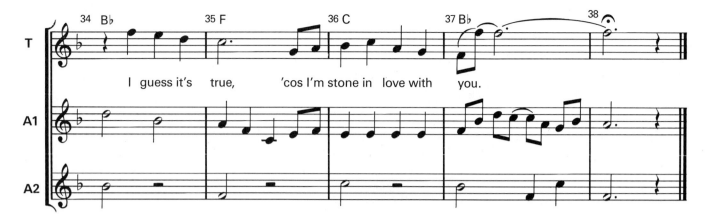

I guess it's true, 'cos I'm stone in love with you.

3   I'd like to someday be the owner of the first house on the moon,
    There would be no neighbours and no population boom,
    You might say that all I do is dream my life away,
    I guess it's true 'Cos I'm stone in love with you'

Ideas

1 Learn to play this arrangement.
2 Perform this song as an instrumental piece. Play it through three times using
   different instruments to play the tune, A1 and A2 in each case. You could play
   part of the tune on one instrument and the rest of it on another. How many
   combinations of tone-colour can you make?
3 Rehearse an instrumental and singing performance of *I'm stone in love with
   you*. Choose several singers to perform the song with a simple kind of dance
   routine.
4 Arrange the chords used in this song into a new chord progression.
   a Play the chord progression through several times.
   b Make up a tune to fit the chord progression. Change instruments or singer
      to provide variety in tone-colour. Play the tune on a lower sounding instru-
      ment and then on a higher sounding instrument.
   c Make up some words for the tune.
   d Make up a bass riff using the notes in each of the accompanying chords.
   e Add some rhythm parts for percussion.
   f Tape record the song you have made up.
5 Listen to several records by a soul performer you like. Try writing a paragraph
   about his or her style as part of the information given on a record sleeve.
6 Listen to several soul records and answer these questions.
   a Are the lyrics about love or another subject?
   b If a man is singing is he singing *falsetto*?
   c Can you hear any singing in harmony?
   d Do you hear the effect of *call and response*?
   e Do you hear any one-syllabled words sung to several notes?
   f Is there a repetitive chorus?
   g Do you hear the trumpet, french horn, trombone, saxophone or flute
      playing?
   h Is there a *coda* at the end of the record?

Recommended listening

Closer Than Close   The Stylistics
Thriller   Michael Jackson
Hotter Than July   Stevie Wonder

ROCK 'n' ROLL

Elvis Presley — the king of rock'n' roll

In the 1950s an explosion of sound known as **rock'n' roll** began in America and became popular with young people all over the world. Influenced by both country and western music and rhythm and blues, rock'n' roll was raw, rebellious music with a new and exciting sound. At the time it was revolutionary because it provided such a contrast to the crooning love songs with sentimental orchestral accompaniments which had previously been popular. There are several features of rock'n' roll's style which account for its special sound, the way it is sung, its lyrics, how and on what instruments it is played as well as its rhythm.

The rock'n' roll sound

The raw-edged sound of rock'n' roll was caused by the use of amplified guitars, screaming saxophones and a powerful beat. Rock'n' roll singers matched the instrumental sound with a wild vocal style. Bill Haley shouts above the backing in *Rock around the clock*, for example, and singers often sounded hoarse and gravelly. Singing techniques included stuttering, hiccuping, growling and wailing. *Heartbreak Hotel* provides a good example of Elvis Presley's particularly expressive and flexible voice. In mid-sentence he changes rhythms effortlessly without appearing to take a breath and sings with ease both low and high notes.

The lyrics

Rock'n' roll was for young people and the song lyrics reflected their interests. *Blue suede shoes* referred to fashions of the day, while many songs were about school as in Chuck Berry's *School's out* and *High school confidential* by Bill Haley. Even food fads became subjects of records, for example, in Elvis Presley's *Hot Dog*. The lyrics were simple and lines were short and often rhyming. There was a tendency to make everything rhyme, even song titles. Take for example *Good golly, Miss Molly* or even *See you later alligator*, the Bill Haley song featured in this topic. Chuck Berry especially liked the words in his songs to rhyme, and he sang them in a rhythmical way. Another trend in rock'n' roll was to include nonsense syllables as part of the lyrics, such as 'oodley pop a cow pop a cow pop a cow cow' or 'dom be do be' and 'be-bop a lula'.

The instruments

The usual combinations of rock'n' roll groups included acoustic or amplified guitars, drums, double bass, banjo, piano and the saxophone. Rock'n' roll was accessible as songs were simple and used only a few chords, while instruments were fairly cheap and relatively easy to play. For example, only five or six musicians played in Bill Haley's group The Comets. In the early 1950s such a limited number of players in a backing group was a novel idea and encouraged many young people to form groups and make records.

In between verses in a rock'n' roll song there would often be an instrument-only section. The piano, guitar or saxophone would play a solo whilst the other instruments accompanied, keeping the bass, rhythm and beat going. Particular effects occurred in these instrument-only sections, for example, the rapid alternation of two notes, known as a **tremolo**, on either the guitar or the piano, or else a number of notes played in rapid succession called a **glissando**. Sometimes the instruments would be played in an outrageous way. One of The Comets used to lie on the floor to play the double bass, while Jerry Lee Lewis occasionally jumped on to the piano or played it with his feet.

double bass

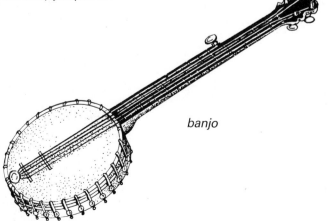

piano

banjo

saxophone

See you later Alligator

Bill Haley and his Comets

Bill Haley and The Comets were originally a country and western group. They experimented by playing with a strong beat on bass and drums and using loud amplified guitars, and came up with a rock'n' roll sound. Popular hits by The Comets were *Shake, rattle and roll*, *Rock a' beatin' boogie* and *See you later, alligator*. The last is a typical rock'n' roll record in several ways. For example, it has four beats in a bar and the *second* and *fourth* beats are accented. It also uses only three chords and each chord is repeated to make a twelve-bar chord pattern as follows:

1 C / / / 2 C / / / 3 C / / / 4 C / / / 5 C / / / 6 F / / /
7 F / / / 8 C / / / 9 C / / / 10 G / / / 11 G / / / 12 C / / /

A2 is a familiar rock'n' roll bass pattern. It is an easy pattern to work out, especially on the xylophone or the piano. The bass is built on the chords shown above the tune. For example, if the chord shown is C the first three notes you play on the piano will be:

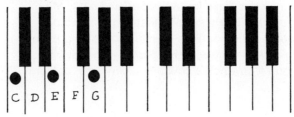

One note is missing so far and this can be found by counting six notes from the root of the chord.

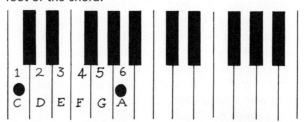

The completed bass pattern is made up of these notes:

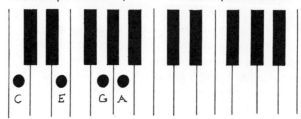

Often in rock'n' roll music each *sung* line is answered by a short tune played on the saxophone, piano or guitar. These answering tunes are the responsibility of A1 players in this arrangement. Remember to stress accented notes.

Suggested instrumertation

Tune Descant recorder, soprano metallophone, xylophone and melodica and glockenspiel.

A1 Descant recorder, alto or tenor xylophones and metallophones, guitar or flute.

A2 Cello, bass guitar, bass xylophone or metallophone.

See you later, alligator

3. I said, wait a minute, 'gator
So you meant it just for play
I said wait a minute, 'gator
So you meant it just for play
Don't you know you really hurt me
This is what I have to say.

Repeat Chorus.

Ideas

1 Learn to sing and play this arrangement.
2 Choose some people to play the appropriate chords as they occur in the arrangement. They can be played on the piano, guitar or shared between two or three xylophones. The chords could be played on the first beat of the bar as follows:

Or they can be played to the rhythm of the first four bars of A1 like this:

3 Experiment with other rhythms to which the chords could be played.
4 Play through the following chord pattern.

G 1	/	/	/	G 2	/	/	/	G 3	/	/	/	G 4	/	/	/
C 5	/	/	/	C 6	/	/	/	G 7	/	/	/	G 8	/	/	/
D 9	/	/	/	C 10	/	/	/	G 11	/	/	/	G 12	/	/	/

a Work out a bass part similar to or the same as the one in *See you later, alligator*.
b Make up a tune for the chord pattern and write some lyrics.
c Invent a rhyming title for your completed song.

5 Listen to any record(s) by Bill Haley and The Comets and then try to answer these questions.
a Can you hear a bass part similar to the one you have played in this arrangement?
b What instrument is playing the bass part?
c Is the beat clear or not?
d Are the second and fourth beats accented?
e Are there any instrumental sections?
f If so, what instruments play solos in these sections?
g In *See you later, alligator* the tune for the verse is the same as the tune for the chorus. In the record you are listening to is the tune of the verse different from or the same as the chorus tune?
h How many *different* chords can you hear in this record?

Recommended listening

Bill Haley and The Comets   *Rock around the clock*.

Memphis, Tennessee

Chuck Berry, who wrote the music and lyrics of Memphis, Tennessee

Chuck Berry wrote the lyrics and the music of nearly all of his songs and many of them have become rock'n' roll classics, including *Roll over Beethoven, Johnny B. Goode, Maybelline, Too much monkey business, Rock'n' music roll* and *Memphis, Tennessee.* As a good guitarist, Chuck Berry's singing and guitar work are almost equally important in their contribution to the overall sound. The piano and drums are sometimes used as additional backing instruments to combine with the piercing sound of the electric guitar.

Many guitarists have been influenced by the introductory phrases, short tunes, chords and bass patterns which he played. A1 demonstrates a common accompanying tune built on the root of the chord and the *fifth* and *sixth* notes from the root. The chord in Bar 1 is D and the accompanying tune in A1 uses the notes just described. For example:

	Root 1	2	3	4	5	6				
C	D	E	F	G	A	B	C	D	E	F
	•				•	•				

In Bar 2 the accompanying tune uses the same notes only this time based on the chord of C. For example:

Root 1	2	3	4	5	6				
C	D	E	F	G	A	B	C	D	E	F
•				•	•				

Although this song is in the key of D major the seventh note of the scale, which is C sharp,

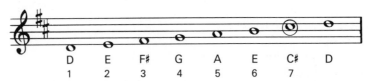

D	E	F#	G	A	E	C#	D
1	2	3	4	5	6	7	

is played as a C natural.

C

It is common in pop music to flatten the seventh note of a scale.

Suggested instrumentation

Tune Soprano melodica, metallophone or xylophone, descant recorder, piano, guitar, glockenspiel and violin.

A1 Descant recorder, guitar, piano, alto or tenor xylophones and metallophones.

A2 Bass guitar, lower range of piano and bass xylophone or metallophone.

Memphis, Tennessee

3. Help me information, more than that I cannot add,
   Only that I miss her and all the fun we had,
   But we were pulled apart, because her Mum did not agree
   And tore apart our happy home in Memphis, Tennessee.

4. Last time I saw Marie, she's waving me goodbye,
   With hurry home drops on her cheek that trickled from her eye.
   Marie is only six years old, information please,
   Try to put me through to her in Memphis, Tennessee.

Ideas

1 Learn to play and sing this song.
2 Create a new bass part for A2 using the notes in the given chords. For instance, the first two bars could be:

3 Make up your own accompanying tune to play instead of the one given in A1. Use only the root of the chord and the *fifth* and *sixth* notes from the root. You can use only three possible notes for each chord but see how many versions you can make up.
4 Play the chords on the guitar and piano or spread the notes in each chord amongst several xylophones.
5 Perform *Memphis, Tennessee* combining singing and playing. Include two instrument-only sections in your performance featuring a different solo instrument each time.
6 Include the effects of *tremolo* and *glissando* in your performances of this song. A tremolo is easily made on a xylophone or glockenspiel by using two beaters and gently alternating each beater on the same note. A glissando can be produced on the xylophone or glockenspiel by sliding a beater quickly across the bars from one end of the instrument to the other. On the piano run your finger along the length of the keyboard.
7 On any instrument play through each of the following rhythms several times. These rhythms frequently occur in rock'n' roll music.

a Now listen to any record by Chuck Berry, Bill Haley or Jerry Lee Lewis. Can you hear any of the rhythms you have just played? If so, write down the appropriate number of the rhythm(s) you can hear.
8 Listen again to some rock'n' roll songs by Chuck Berry, Bill Haley or Jerry Lee Lewis and answer these questions.
   a What instruments accompany the song?
   b Write down the words of one verse. Do the words rhyme?
   c How many choruses are there and how many verses?
   d Can you hear an instrumental section?
   e In a rock'n' roll record the backing occasionally stops after accompanying one word in each line. Do you notice this effect?
   f Did you hear a glissando?

Recommended listening

Motorvatin'   Chuck Berry
The Original Jerry Lee Lewis   Jerry Lee Lewis

Wooden Heart

Elvis Presley in concert, country 'n' western style

Elvis Presley, affectionately known as 'The King', was the most important singer to emerge during the 1950s. He was equally comfortable singing both hard driving numbers such as *Jailhouse Rock*, *Lawdy Miss Clawdy* or *Hound Dog* as well as country and western-inspired songs like *You're right, I'm left, she's gone* and *Mystery train*. He also sang romantic pop songs such as *Blue Moon*, *Love me tender* and *Wooden Heart*. Singing in such a varied range of styles made him popular with a wide audience and he was the first singer to have a series of million-selling singles.

Wooden Heart was recorded in 1961 at a time when romantic songs had become fashionable again. This song is in a different mood from *See you later, Alligator* and *Memphis, Tennessee*. Try and make your singing and playing of *Wooden Heart* as expressive as possible by sometimes getting softer and sometimes getting louder.

A 'getting softer' sign in music looks like this

A 'getting louder' sign in music looks like this

This song is in *three* sections.

First section Main tune, Bars 4-23
Second section New tune, Bars 24-31
Third section Main tune, Bars 32-42.

Suggested instrumentation

Tune Glockenspiel, violin, descant recorder, soprano melodica, xylophone, metallophone and guitar.

A1 Alto melodica, alto or tenor metallophones and xylophones as well as the guitar.

A2 Bass guitar, cello, lower range of piano and bass xylophone or metal-lophone.

You could change instruments playing the tune and A1 between bars 24 and 31 to highlight the new tune and accompanying material if you like.

Wooden Heart

Ideas

1 Learn to play and sing this song.
2 Make up a rhythmic accompaniment using only *untuned* percussion. Give each instrument a different rhythm to play.
For example:

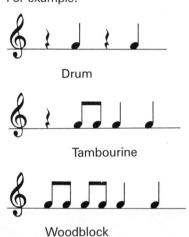

Drum

Tambourine

Woodblock

3 Experiment with the speed of your performance. Play it fast, at a medium speed and slowly.
4 Tape record the performances at each different speed so you can listen and decide which speed you prefer.
5 Divide into groups and rehearse this arrangement.
   a Tape record each group's version of this song.
   b Give your group an imaginary name.
   c Select a panel of judges who will judge each performance on how expressively it was played.
6 Make up an imaginary list of Top Ten rock'n' roll records. Include the names of the rock'n' roll stars who recorded them.
7 Listen to several of Elvis Presley's records. His singing was very often supported by a vocal backing group called The Jordanaires. Answer the following questions.
   a Do you hear any supporting vocals?
   b Write down some of the words or phrases on which they sing with Presley.
   c Do they sing the same tune or a slightly different one?
   d Do they sing to nonsense syllables? If so, what are the ones they use?
   e Do the vocals ever reply to Presley's singing by immediately repeating what he has just sung?
8 Listen to other Presley records and answer these questions.
   a Describe the introductions of these records.
   b In your opinion, is the speed of the record fast, medium or slow?
   c Does the music ever slow down, get faster, louder or softer? If you hear any of these, say which you have heard.
   d Can you hear an example of *tremolo* on the piano, guitar or drums?
   e How does the record end?
9 Compare two of Presley's records. In what ways are they similar and in what ways do they differ?

Recommended listening

The Sun Collection   Elvis Presley
40 Greatest, Elvis Presley   Elvis Presley RCA PL42691(2)

CLASSICAL

18th-century chamber music with singer, harpsichord, flute and strings

Classical music

Baroque   1650-1750

Classical period   1750-1830

Romantic   1830-late 19th century

At a **classical** concert you listen to music which might be anything from 20 to 300 years old. The term 'classical' has two meanings. When people talk of classical music they might mean music which has lasted and not gone out of fashion as is the case with some kinds of pop music. Or they could be referring to music written between 1750 and 1830. You are probably familiar with more classical music than you think. Nowadays, classical music is often used in films, as title music to television programmes or even in radio advertisements. Sometimes, classical tunes are borrowed and made into pop tunes or become the basis of another kind of music altogether. Many of the classics have been given a soul beat and are played in a funky way.

As with clothes, there are also fashions in music. Purcell, Beethoven and Brahms were each influenced by the musical trends of the time in which they wrote their music. It will help you to understand the music of these composers and their contemporaries to know something about these musical fashions.

Baroque

Purcell wrote music in the **Baroque** period. During this time rich and important people began to take a greater interest in music and were willing to employ composers to make up music for special occasions.

Colourful ceremonies called for impressive sound and therefore music was written in strong rhythms, featuring blaring trumpets and thundering drum rolls. Rhythmic music with a clear, steady beat was also in demand to accompany the popular courtly dances of the day. The effect of **contrast** is used a lot in the compositions of Purcell and other Baroque composers. Musical differences or contrasts are highlighted in several ways. For instance, different speeds, tone colours and rhythms are *contrasted*; a slow section immediately follows a fast section; the sound of a few instruments alternates with new and often larger combinations of instruments; smooth sounding rhythms contrast with jagged ones. The bass part was considered very important and would be played on early keyboard instruments like the clavier or harpsichord.

Classical

Haydn, Mozart and Beethoven, the most famous composers of the **Classical** period, were kept busy writing **symphonies** to cater for public demand. A symphony is a piece written for a combined collection of string, wind, brass and percussion instruments known as an **orchestra**. In the Classical period people started to listen and concentrate on music. Composers took care to give their music variety and yet use enough repetition so that audiences became familiar with certain tunes as they listened.

A symphony is divided in three or four main contrasting sections or **movements** and each varies in mood and speed. To grab the listener's attention there are moments of surprise, sudden drops from a loud volume to a soft one, or abrupt changes of mood and unexpected pauses or silences. The addition of the clarinet and french horn to the orchestra gave composers scope to experiment with new combinations of sound.

Wolfgang Amadeus Mozart (1756-1791): Austrian composer

Romantic

During the **Romantic** period composers wrote music that expressed their own individuality. New chords were introduced to music and mechanically improved instruments covered a wide range of sounds. Composers asked for instruments to be played in novel ways to create particular tone-colours. In fact, during this period there was much interest in sound possibilities and parts were written for unusual combinations of instruments. The orchestra grew larger and included new instruments such as the low-toned tuba and high-sounding piccolo and the harp. There was also less concern with rhythm and a greater interest in inventing beautiful tunes or melodies.

Franz Joseph Haydn (1732-1809): Austrian composer

Minuet

This Minuet by Purcell is taken from a set of short dance pieces. These dance sets are known as **suites**. The Minuet is clearly divided into two sections and each section is to be played twice. The repeats were essential as the dance steps fitted the tunes exactly and if each section was not repeated the dancers would very likely end up with their partners out of reach. At the end of each section the dancers would nod briefly or curtsey to their partners.

Minuets are written with three beats in a bar and the tunes fall into two bar **phrases**. A phrase is a short tune made up of several notes. When you listen to the tune of this Minuet you will hear a slight break after every two bars. This break marks the end of a phrase. Phrases are shown on written music by a curved line which reaches from the note beginning the phrase to the note ending it like this;

A tune without phrase marks is like a sentence without punctuation. Phrases can vary in length but in the Minuet they are short to match the small dancing steps.

*Henry Purcell (1659–1695):
English composer*

Suggested instrumentation

Tune Flute, violin, descant recorder, oboe, soprano metallophone or xylophone.

A1 Descant recorder, violin, alto or tenor xylophones.

A2 Cello, bass xylophone or metallophone.

A Minuet by Purcell

Ideas

1 Learn to play this arrangement.

2 Composers in Purcell's time liked to contrast the sound of a small group of instruments with the sound of a larger group of instruments. Have a small group of instruments play each repeated section.

3 A favourite pastime in 1766 (according to a music magazine of the period) was making up short dance pieces. Readers were given this advice: sound the chord of C followed by the chord of G, give each chord three beats:

Repeat this four times. Make up a tune which sounds good over the given chords. Divide it into two and repeat each section. Try and make up a Minuet in this way.

4 Compose a tune which clearly falls into two-bar phrases. Play it to a member of your class and ask if they can hear where each phrase ends.

5 Make up a piece of *contrasts*. Here are some suggestions; loud/soft, fast/slow, smooth/jagged rhythms, high/low sounds, untuned/tuned percussion instruments.

6 Listen to some music by the Baroque composers, Bach, Vivaldi or Handel and answer these questions.

   a Do you notice a contrast between the sound of a larger and a smaller group of instruments playing?

   b Do you hear the same tune being played by one instrument and then on a different kind?

   c Does the rhythm stay virtually the same throughout the time you listen?

   d Can you hear a high-sounding tune being played with a low-sounding tune?

7 In the Baroque period the bass part of a piece of music was very important. Purcell liked the sound of the bass so much he would make up a piece of music based entirely on a short repeated bass tune. This kind of bass tune was called a **ground bass**.

   a Learn to play this ground bass by Purcell.

   b Now learn to play the same ground bass starting on the note G.

   c Listen to 'The Triumphing Dance' from Purcell's *Dido and Aeneas*. Concentrate on the ground bass as you listen. It is repeated three times before it is played on the new note G. Then it is played another three times starting on C and then stops. How many bars does it stop for?

Recommended listening

Dido and Aeneas (The Triumphing Dance)   Purcell
The Brandenburg Concertos (nos 1, 2, 4 and 5)   J.S. Bach
The Water Music   Handel
The Four Seasons   Vivaldi

Sonatina

In Beethoven's day the shape or **form** of a piece of music was very important. A composer made up a piece of music with a plan or form already in mind. The form of a *Sonatina* was often used by composers in the Classical period. The music falls into three sections. The first and third sections are either the same or else very similar. In this Sonatina however they are exactly the same and begin with this tune.

The second section would be related to the first yet different enough to provide a contrast. Often, as is the case with this Sonatina the music ends with a coda.

The *form* looks like this:

first section

second section

third section

coda

Ludwig van Beethoven (1770–1827): German composer

The kind of accompaniment which occurs in this piece can frequently be heard in music of the Classical period. There was a tendency to split the notes of a chord into the kind of pattern shared between A1 and A2 in bars 5 and 6 and between bars 25 to 31.

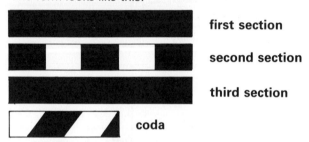

This kind of chord note pattern is called an **alberti bass**.

Suggested instrumentation

Tune Piano, soprano xylophone, metallophone and glockenspiel.
A1   Alto melodica, piano, or alto and tenor metallophone and xylophone.
A2   Cello, bass xylophone or metallophone.

Haydn, Mozart and Beethoven were most particular about dynamics so make sure you play with all the loud, soft, getting louder and getting softer markings.

f = loud
p = soft

Sonatina by Beethoven

Ideas

1 Learn to play this arrangement.
2 Share the tune between two groups of the same instruments by each group playing every other phrase. Take care to make it sound as if only one group is playing it.
3 To draw attention to the second section you can change the instruments playing the tune to the recorder or give the tune to a solo player.
4 Can you say why the second section of this Sonatina is similar to the first and third sections and yet different from them?
5 Make up a piece of music in three sections.
6 Create some music using instrumental and vocal sounds using a wide range of *dynamics*. Include sounds which are very loud, loud, medium loud, soft, very soft and also some moments in the music which get louder or softer.
7 Choose three different chords and make up your own *alberti bass* accompaniment. The notes in a chord can be arranged in any order. For example, here is the chord of F arranged in three different *alberti* patterns.

8 Listen to a Beethoven symphony. Do you notice any of the following moments of surprise?
   a sudden drop from very loud to very soft.
   b lots of instruments suddenly followed by a few.
   c abrupt changes in speed.
   d unexpected pauses or silences.
9 Haydn liked to include a Minuet in the symphonies he wrote. These Minuets were in three sections with the first and third sections either the same or very similar. Listen to a Minuet from a Haydn symphony and answer these questions.
   a As the first section is being played feel the beat and count in threes. When it is repeated how many bars are there in the first section?
   b Is the second section played on the same combination of instruments?
   c Is the third section exactly the same as the first or slightly different?
10 Compare the first few minutes of Beethoven's Symphony No. 5 with the funky version played on the record *Hooked on Classics*. Can you think of two differences?

Recommended listening

Symphonies   Beethoven
Symphonies (nos 13, 14, 15, 20, 21, 22, 30 and 40)   Haydn
Hooked On Classics   K-TEL 1146

Variations on a theme of Haydn.

Theme and Variations is another kind of musical plan a composer uses to give shape to a piece of music. In this type of form a composer takes a simple tune or **theme** and repeats it many times. Each time the tune or theme is repeated it is played in a different way. The composer varies the theme by changing the speed, rhythm, mood, accompaniment or the key the theme was first heard in.

This theme which Brahms borrowed from Haydn is in three parts with a short coda at the end. In each of the Variations the plan of the theme remains the same. There are eight Variations of the theme before a final closing section. In this last section Brahms uses a **ground bass** just as Purcell used to do and each time the ground bass is heard the accompanying music is changed.

Johannes Brahams (1833–1897): German composer

Suggested instrumentation

Tune Violin, flute, descant recorder, soprano metallophone, xylophone or metallophone, guitar and piano.

A1 Descant recorder, violin, alto or tenor xylophones and metallophones.

A2 Cello, bass xylophone or metallophone and bass guitar.

Variations on a Theme of Haydn (The Theme)

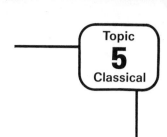
Ideas

1 Learn to play this arrangement.
2 Divide into groups. Each group can make their own variation of this theme. Keep the theme the same but change the accompaniment. Here are some suggestions.

   a Accompany the tune with suitable rhythms on untuned percussion instruments.

   b Play the accompanying chords in a reggae rhythm by sounding them on the second and fourth quaver beats of a bar like this:

   c Keep changing the instrument which plays the tune. There are many other ways to vary it.

   d When each group has worked out a variation, play the given arrangement as a class and then listen to each group's variation in turn.

3 Composers in the 20th century often choose a musical idea rather than a tune as the inspiration for a set of variations. Try and think of your own musical idea and make up a few variations on it. You could choose five notes and then play them in as many ways as you can. Or, experiment with vocal sounds or even decide on a series of instrumental sounds and then re-arrange their order.

4 Follow the theme through as you listen to Brahms's *Orchestral Variations on a theme by Haydn*. Answer these questions:

   a Is the tune always played on the same instruments?

   b Listen out for the dynamics. Can you say which bars are played softly and which bars sound louder?

5 Listen to Brahms's first variation. What can you hear that reminds you of the theme?

6 Play through the ground bass used in the final closing section of Brahms's Variations.

7 Listen to the final closing section. How many times is this ground bass played?

   a Does it always sound on deep or low notes or is it ever heard on higher sounding instruments?

   b How many times do you hear the ground bass before the theme is heard again?

Recommended listening

Variations on a Theme By Haydn (Orchestral version)   Brahms
Variations for Flute and Electronic Sounds   Walter Carlos
Atmospheres   György Ligeti
Sonata in A major (First movement)   Mozart

JAZZ

Duke Ellington's 'front line'

The famous jazz musician Louis Armstrong once said that if people have to ask what jazz is 'they are never going to know'. The way to understand jazz is to listen to it and become familiar with its sound. Here are some special features to look out for when you play or listen to jazz.

Improvisation

Jazz musicians often take a simple two or three part tune and use it to make up music 'on the spot' in performance. When a musician makes up music during a performance it is called **improvising**. Jazz players might improvise around a City Blues tune such as *Mama don't allow it*, or a popular song from the 1930s like *Ol' Man Mose* or even a jazzy song like *It don't mean a thing* written by Duke Ellington.

Syncopation

A jazz player must also be able to **swing** as well as improvise. Jazz is music which
swings. It makes you want to tap your feet when you listen. Other kinds of music
like rock'n' or soul can swing, but in jazz it is a special quality of its rhythm. The
beat in jazz is at a steady speed and performers are always aware of it as they play
or sing contrasting swung rhythms. **Syncopation** is part of what gives a jazz
performance this swing. A drummer playing Classical music would sound this

rhythm ♩ 4/4 ♩♩♩♩, *BOOM chick BOOM chick* and in doing so would accent

the strong beats which are the first and third beats in a bar. A jazz drummer will
naturally play *boom CHICK boom CHICK* and shift the accent from the strong
to the weak beats. When sounds which are not normally stressed are accented, a
rhythmic effect known as syncopation is created. Here are three examples which
can be found in *Ol' Man Mose*, *Mama don't allow it* and *It don't mean a thing*.

1 There can be a longer note on a weak beat.

2 A rest on a strong beat.

3 A tie over the first strong beat.

Solo breaks and scat singing

Jazz musicians place a great deal of importance on developing their own individual
sound and style; two trumpeters can sound very different particularly when they
improvise a solo **break**. To improvise a solo without any accompaniment is known
as a break. Certain tone-colours are especially associated with the jazz sound.
Instrumentalists like to imitate vocal sounds and this accounts for *screams*, *bends*,
scoops, *squeaks* and *slurs* and also the use of vibrato often heard in solo breaks.
Jazz singers sometimes use their voices as if they were instruments and Louis
Armstrong popularised a type of wordless vocal improvisation kown as **scat**
singing.

The instruments of jazz

The instrumentalists in a traditional jazz group function as either **front-line** or
rhythm section players. Front-line instruments play the tune or harmonies, improvise breaks and include the saxophone, clarinet, trombone and trumpet. The
accompanying rhythm section is made up of the tuba, banjo, piano, drums or
double bass.

   To perform the following arrangements in the right style you will need to listen
to some jazz records to catch the swing feeling.

75

Mama don't allow it

Billie Holiday, one of the great jazz singers of the 30s and 40s.

Mama don't allow it was recorded by, amongst others, Julia Lee, whose humorous and individual singing style was influenced by great City Blues singers such as Ma Rainey, Bessie Smith and Billie Holiday.

This song was often used to introduce the players in a jazz group. At the end of a verse, the instrument mentioned (as in, for example, 'Mama don't allow no piano players in here') would demonstrate his skills by improvising a break.

If you listen to the tune you will hear a long held note at the end of the first, second and fourth phrases. These long notes provide a 'space' in the music for front-line players to improvise short fill-in tunes which are made up around the notes in the accompanying chords.

Mama don't allow it also features the use of **blue notes**. Blue notes are found by flattening the third and seventh notes of a major scale. This tune is composed in the key of C and the blue notes are;

C	D	E♭	F	G	A	B♭	C
1	2	3	4	5	6	7	8

Add the *blue* notes of E and B flat to any tuned percussion instrument playing this tune. Stress any accented weak beats to create a syncopated effect.

Chords can be built on any note. In this song they are easy to find as they are built on the *first*, *fourth* and *fifth* notes of a scale:

```
G           C   D
E           A   B
C   D   E   F   G   A   B   C
1   2   3   4   5   6   7   8
```

Suggested instrumentation

Tune Violin, oboe, glockenspiel, piano, guitar, soprano melodica, metallophone or xylophone.

A1 Descant recorder, alto melodica, alto and tenor xylophone or metal-lophone.

A2 Bass guitar, lower range of piano and bass xylophone or metallophone.

Mama Don't Allow It

ma-ma don't al-low no mu-sic played in here.

Mama don't allow no piano players in here.
Mama don't allow no piano players in here.
Though you were of Paderewski fame
She still would put you in the 'Hall of Shame',
'Cause Mama don't allow no piano players in here.

Mama don't allow no slap-bass play'rs in here.
Mama don't allow no slap-bass play'rs in here.
My mam claims it really is a sin
To play upon a swollen violin;
So Mama don't allow no slap-bass play'rs in here.

Mama don't allow no guitar players in here.
Mama don't allow no guitar players in here.
Makes no diff'rence if you're flat or sharp.
You're gonna wake up playin' on a harp;
'Cause Mama don't allow no guitar players in here.

Mama don't allow no saxophones in here.
Mama don't allow no saxophones in here;
Ev'ry time she listens to a sax,
She feels so good, she pays her income tax;
So Mama don't allow no saxophones in here.

Mama don't allow no drummer man in here,
Mama don't allow no drummer man in here,
Mama says you're gonna go 'boom',
If she should catch you drummin' in this room,
'Cause Mama don't allow no drummer man in here.

Mama don't allow no nothin' done in here,
Mama don't allow no nothin' done in here,
Don't know how I'll ever get along,
'Cause when I'm doin 'nothin', somethin's wrong,
But Mama don't allow no nothin' done in here.

Ideas

1 Play this arrangement.

2 Work on your own and make up two *fill-ins*. The first should be made up around

the notes in the chord of C6 | C | D | E | F | G | A | B | C | D | E | F |

so that it can be played in bars 7 and 8. The second should use the notes in

the chord of G7 | C | D | E | F | G | A | B | C | D | E | F | and be

played with bars 11 and 12.

3 Perform the arrangement as a class. Choose a leader who can indicate during the performance which players should add a fill-in at appropriate times.

4 Change the words of the song to match the instruments you are playing.

5 Sing the song incorporating several solo breaks at the end of verses to match the words as you have changed them.

6 Write some lyrics for a song using the same formula as *Mama don't allow it* two repeated lines followed by two different ones and then another repetition of the first line.

7 Now make up a tune in the key of C to the words you have written and include the *blue* notes.

8 Invent some *syncopated* rhythms in $\frac{4}{4}$ time. You can use the examples given in the introduction to help you.

9 Work in groups and compose a piece of music using the syncopated rhythms you have made up.

10 The blues tune *Careless Love* is in the key of F. Chords built on the first, fourth and fifth notes of the scale of F can accompany this tune. The chords are F, B♭ and C. Apart from the first bar there is a chord change every four beats. Find the chord which suits each of the remaining bars. The notes in the tune give you clues, for example, in Bar 2 the note is F. The chords of F and B♭ include this note. Play each chord in turn with Bar 2 until you decide which one sounds best.

Careless love

11 Work out a simple accompaniment and then perform *Careless love*.

12 The blues are written in a variety of moods about many different subjects. Listen to several blues records. Write down briefly what they are about, and whether you find them sad, happy, angry or humorous.

13 Listen again to a blues record. How many phrases can you hear in each verse? Do you hear any fill-in tunes?

Recommended listening

The Golden Years Vols 1 and 2   Billie Holliday
The Worlds Greatest Blues Singer   Bessie Smith
Tonight's The Night   Julia Lee
(including Mama don't allow it)

Ol' man Mose

During the 1930s Louis Armstrong liked to think of himself as an entertainer as well as a musician. His performances included not only trumpet playing and singing, but also clowning around in front of the audience. *Ol' Man Mose* was composed, sung and played by him at this stage of his career and is a light-hearted song in three sections. The words are not meant to be taken seriously.

You will notice many seventh chords in this song. They are widely used in jazz along with the *sixth chord* also featured in this arrangement. The sixth chord is a triad with an extra note added to it. It is called a sixth chord because the added note is *six* notes from the root of the chord. Take the chord which occurs in *Ol' Man Mose* as an example. The notes in the triad of D minor are:

C	D•	E	F•	G	A•	B	C	D	E	F

Now count up six notes from the root of the chord.

C	D	E	F	G	A	B•	C	D	E	F
	1	2	3	4	5	6				

You come to B and the chord of D minor 6 is

C	D•	E	F•	G	A•	B•	C	D	E	F

Remember this is a good humoured song. Play A1 and A2 with a lot of bounce.

Emphasize the syncopated rhythm ♩ ♩ ♩ in A1. As all parts in the first eight bars are quite busy allow the tune to be heard above A1 and A2.

Louis Armstrong, one of the most famous of all jazz trumpeters

---

Suggested instrumentation

Tune Violin, flute, oboe, descant recorder, glockenspiel, guitar, piano, soprano xylophone and metallophone.

A1 Alto or tenor metallophone and xylophone, violin, piano and alto melodica.

A2 Bass guitar, cello and bass xylophone or metallophone.

Ol' Man Mose

Ideas

1 Learn to play this arrangement.
2 Invent some rhythms to play on untuned percussion such as the tambourine, cymbal and drum. Pay attention to the words so that your rhythms add an appropriate atmosphere.
3 Learn to sing the song.
4 Sing A1 from bar 3 to 18 as a harmony part to the tune. Sing it to some nonsense syllables, for example, *doo bah doo*, which match the rhythm.

   doo bah doo
5 When you sing *Ol' Man Mose* try and bring out the humour in the words as much as possible.
   a You could split the words in the chorus between two groups or divide them between a solo and chorus group.
   b Shout, speak or whisper certain words in the song to surprise the listener or emphasize the lyrics.
6 If you especially like singing, decide how you would perform this song. You might like to sing one of the verses in *scat* fashion.
7 Work on your own and make up a variation of the chorus tune of *Ol' Man Mose*. Some suggestions: change the rhythm, miss out some notes, add some notes or play some new ones. Play your chorus in a performance of *Ol' Man Mose*.
8 Work out the notes in the following sixth chords: C6, F6 and G6.
   a Divide into groups of four. Each take one note of every chord. Arrange these chords in an order you like the sound of. Use them to make up a piece of music.
   b Test each other to find out if you can hear when a chord has the *sixth* note from its root added and when it does not.
9 Work out the tune *When the saints go marching in* starting on C. Create a performance of it in theme and variations form. Introduce the tune, and then make up a number of choruses to be played over the accompaniment before returning to the tune as you originally played it. Divide your instrumentalists into *front-line* and *rhythm section* players.
10 Listen to any of Louis Armstrong's songs. Decide if they are in two or three sections.
   a Can you hear any examples of scat singing?
   b Name or draw the instruments you hear playing a solo and any instruments playing the accompaniment.

Recommended listening

The Louis Armstrong Story   (Four Volumes; Volume 1 includes *Ol' Man Mose*)
Ella and Louis   Ella Fitzgerald and Louis Armstrong
Satchmo   (A musical autobiography of Louis Armstrong)

It don't mean a thing

Duke Ellington was an outstanding jazz composer, pianist and bandleader from 1920 until his death in 1974. He wrote over a thousand tunes and many of them combined with lyrics like *It don't mean a thing* became popular songs.

The two-bar introduction to this song is marked as a **vamp**. A *vamp* is played over and over again until the front-line instruments are ready to play.

A2 is a **walking bass**. This is generally played in a jazz group by a double bass or a bass guitar. A walking bass marks out the beat and by playing important notes from the accompanying chords, outlines the chord progressions in the song. The bass player has two important things to do. In keeping time he creates a steady four beats in a bar background against which the other players can offset their syncopated rhythms. Also in outlining the accompanying chords he helps the other players to hear the notes around which they should improvise.

Duke Ellington at the piano

Suggested instrumentation

Tune Piano, descant recorder, soprano melodica, metallophone or xylophone and violin.

A1 Violin, alto melodica, alto or tenor metallophone or xylophone.

A2 Cello, bass guitar, lower range of piano and bass xylophone or metallophone.

If you play A1 on a metallophone or xylophone you will need both C and C♯ on the instrument.

C	C♯	D	E	F	G	A	B	C	D	E

85

It don't mean a thing

(If it ain't got that swing)

By Duke Ellington and Irving Mills

Ideas

1 Play this arrangement of *It don't mean a thing*.

2 Learn to sing this song. It should be sung rhythmically so emphasize the words or syllables which fall on accented weak beats.

3 Make up a syncopated rhythm which can be played throughout the song as an **ostinato**. An ostinato is a rhythm or tune pattern which is repeated over and over again.

4 Sing a scat version of the tune with A1 and A2 played as an accompaniment.

5 Sing the 'doo-wah' section of this tune in harmony.

6 Jazz too uses the Gospel 'call and response' musical effect. Incorporate call and response ideas in your performance of this song. For example, the first phrase of the tune can be played by one or two instruments making a 'call' and the 'response' can be the second phrase played by a larger group of instruments.

7 Contrasts of tone-colour are important in jazz, for example, the contrast between vocal and instrumental breaks, or short solo exchanges between two instruments. There is also a contrast between the fuller sound of a larger group with the thinner sound of solo players. Listen to a number of jazz records and describe as many contrasts of sound as you can.

8 Listen to a few jazz numbers by Duke Ellington and his Band and answer these questions.
 a Can you hear a walking bass?
 b Write down any examples of call and response effects you hear.

9 Work out your own arrangement of the following tune, *Frankie and Johnny*:

 a Choose players to perform the tune and others to play selected notes from the accompanying chords.
 b Make up a walking bass part.
 c Appoint a band leader to take responsibility for speed, dynamics, variety in tone-colour, starting or ending performances and the balance between tune and accompaniment.
 d Perform *Frankie and Johnny* and try to include at least three choruses.

Recommended listening

The Ellington Era Vol. 1 (including 'It don't mean a thing')
At His Very Best—Duke Ellington and His Orchestra
The Smithsonian Collection of Classic Jazz   Smithsonian

Bb Parts Topic 1

Maid of Orleans

Heart of Gold

Can't stand losing you

B♭ Parts Topic 4

See your later alligator

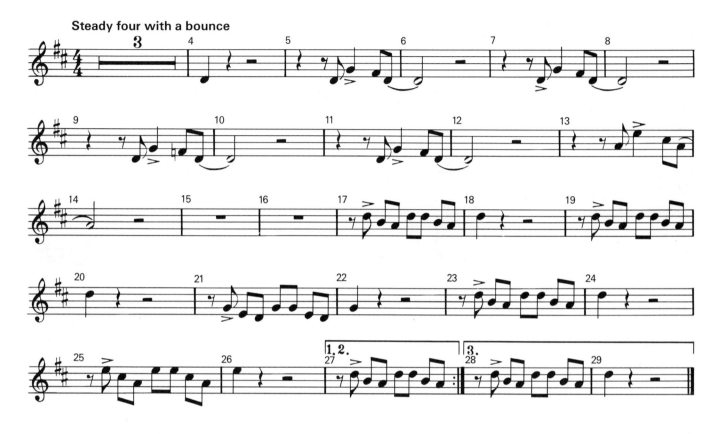

Memphis, Tennessee

Wooden Heart

A Minuet by Purcell

Sonatina by Beethoven

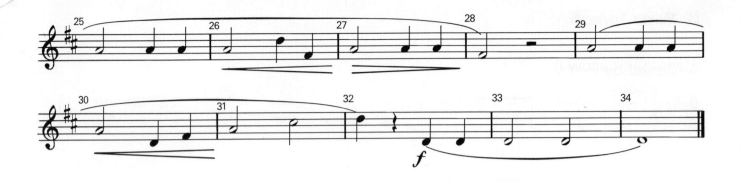

Variations on a Theme of Haydn

Majestically

B♭ Parts Topic 6

Mama don't allow it

Ol' Man Mose

Vamp (Till Ready)

It don't mean a thing